Furniture

Fruit

Parts of the Body

Food and Drinks

Opposites

Special Days

Vegetable

Jobs

Animals

Vehicles

# Der Englisch-Duden

## Erste Wörter – kleine Sätze

von Ute Müller-Wolfangel

und Cornelia Pardall

mit Bildern von Barbara Scholz

**Dudenverlag**

Mannheim · Leipzig · Wien · Zürich

Bibliografische Information der Deutschen Bibliothek
Die Deutsche Bibliothek verzeichnet diese Publikation
in der Deutschen Nationalbibliografie;
detaillierte bibliografische Daten sind im Internet
über http://dnb.ddb.de abrufbar.

Das Wort Duden ist für den Verlag
Bibliographisches Institut & F. A. Brockhaus AG
als Marke geschützt.

Das Werk wurde in neuer Rechtschreibung verfasst.

Redaktion: Katja Schüler
Lektorat: Susanne Klein, Hamburg
Herstellung: Claudia Rönsch
Umschlaggestaltung: Mischa Acker
Satz: Michelle Vollmer, Mainz
Druck und Bindung: Stalling GmbH, Oldenburg

Printed in Germany
ISBN 3-411-70991-x

# Inhalt

# Liebe Eltern, liebe Lehrerinnen und Lehrer,

Mountainbike, Gameboy, Milkshake, ... diese englischen Wörter kennen Kinder aus ihrer unmittelbaren Lebenswelt. Sie benutzen sie ganz selbstverständlich in ihrer täglichen Sprache. An dieses unbefangene Umgehen mit Wörtern aus einer Fremdsprache knüpft der Englisch-Duden an.

Der erste Teil ist in **21 Themengebiete aus dem Erlebnis- und Erfahrungshorizont** von Kindern eingeteilt. Die zu lernenden Wörter werden in Bild und Wort dargestellt. Unten auf der rechten Seite steht zu jedem Thema passend ein Sprachmuster, in das gelernte Wörter der jeweiligen Seiten eingesetzt werden können. Am Ende des ersten Teil sind alle Sprachmuster mit der dazugehörigen deutschen Übersetzung noch einmal aufgelistet.

Im zweiten Teil steht der **aktive Umgang mit der englischen Sprache** im Mittelpunkt. Über Spiele, Lieder und Bildergeschichten lernen die Kinder die englische Sprache aktiv anzuwenden. Die zu den Bildergeschichten dazugehörigen „First Phrases" unterstützen die Verständigung auf Englisch in Alltagssituationen. Im Anschluss an die Bildergeschichten sind diese „First Phrases" auf Deutsch übersetzt.

Der dritte Teil des Englisch-Dudens ist ein **kleines Wörterbuch** zum Nachschlagen. Dort sind alle englischen Wörter des ersten Teils mit Lautschrift alphabetisch geordnet und auf Deutsch übersetzt. Auf der letzten Seite ist eine Lautschrifttabelle abgebildet.

Für alle, die sich auf das Englischlernen freuen, ist der Englisch-Duden ein Anreiz, sich mit der neuen Sprache zu beschäftigen. Für Vorschüler und Schulanfänger ist es eine Möglichkeit, über das Bild die Sprache zu erlernen. Für fortgeschrittene Grundschüler dient er als erstes Nachschlagewerk für die englische Sprache. Damit bietet der Englisch-Duden die Grundlage für das erste Fremdsprachenlernen.

Die Autorinnen

Das ist Nessie, die Leitfigur des Englisch-Dudens.
Sie ist schon ein Englisch-Profi und stellt die Themen vor.

## Benutzerhinweise

### Teil 1

#### 1. Wörter
– das englische Wort vorsprechen und auf das dazugehörige Bild deuten
– Kind das Wort mehrmals nachsprechen und auf das Bild zeigen lassen

#### 2. Sprachmuster
– Satz vorsprechen
– Kind nachsprechen lassen
  (die bildlich dargestellten Wörter durch entsprechende Wörter auf der Seite ersetzen lassen)

### Teil 2

– First Phrases vorsprechen
– Kind nachsprechen lassen
– in „Spiel"situationen die First Phrases anwenden

Buggy

Jeans

Clown

Sweatshirt

cornflakes

Muffi

Chips

Nessie

Milk-shake

Teddy

Mountain-bike

Gameboy

Inline-skates

Discman

6

# Animals

dolphin

penguin

lion

elephant

monkey

bear

tiger

giraffe

sheep

hen

duck

goat

goose

cow

pig

horse

The  lives in the zoo.
The  lives on the farm.

# Pets

bird

mouse

guinea pig

puppy

dog

hamster

rabbit

kitten

cat

parrot

goldfish

turtle

Where is the  ?

Here it is.

# Toys

teddy bear

kite

football

building bricks

jigsaw puzzle

skipping rope

train set

car

play dough

doll

ball

puppet

ghost

witch

cowboy    princess

king

Can I have the ⬛, please?

Here you are.

Yes, you can. / No, you can't.

# Food and Drinks

egg

bread      butter      cheese

salt

lemonade      pepper

juice      mineral water      sugar

ham

sausage

jam

honey

hot chocolate

milk

tea

Pass the 🥖, please.

Here it is.

15

# Fruit

pineapple

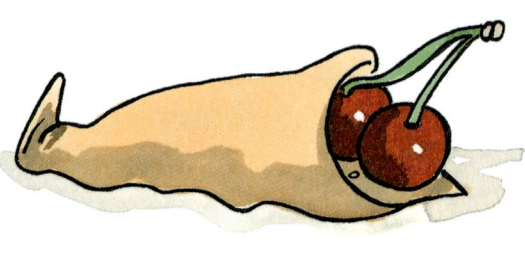

cherries

strawberries

grapes

orange

watermelon

apple

pear

banana

kiwi fruit

plum

peach

lemon

Can I have a , please?
Can I have some , please?
Yes, you can. / No, you can't.

# Vegetable

potato

beans

cabbage

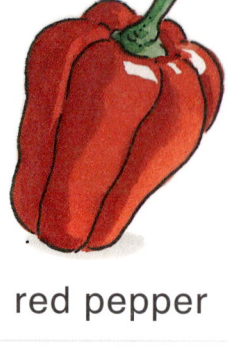

red pepper

radish

onion

cucumber

carrot

lettuce

tomato

mushroom

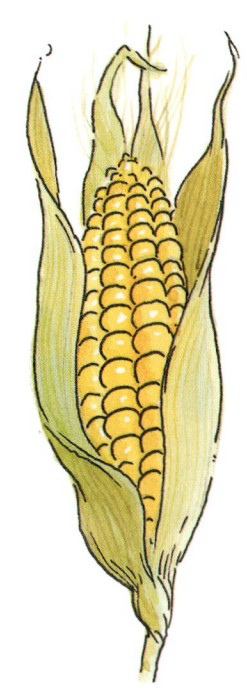

corn

cauliflower

peas

I like eating .

I don't like eating .

# Parts of the body

head

hair

ear

face

mouth

nose

chin

eye

tooth

tongue

neck

finger

hand

shoulder

elbow

arm

body

toe

leg

knee

foot

Show me your !

This is my .

21

# Family

child / children

parents

father

mother

daughter

son

baby

grandparents

grandfather

grandmother

22

twins

aunt

uncle

sister       brother

Do you like your  ?

Yes, I do. / No, I don't.

I don't have a .

23

# Clothes

jacket

shoes

watch

hat

trousers

coat

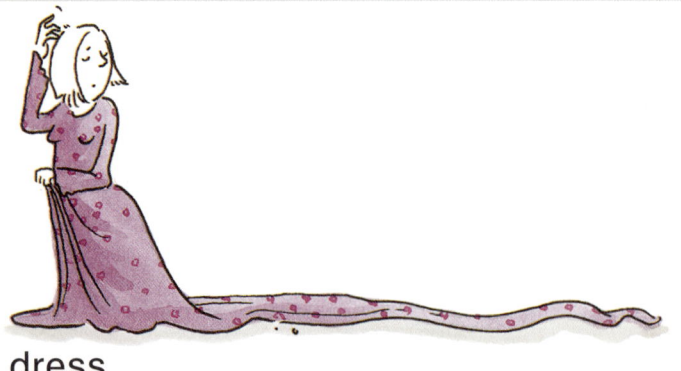

dress

skirt

sunglasses

glasses

cap

shirt          sweater

shorts

boots          socks

I like wearing my .

I don't like wearing my .

# At Home

1 living room
2 kitchen
3 garden
4 bathroom
5 bedroom
6 door
7 toilet
8 stairway
9 window
10 hall

house

spoon

knife

glass

cup

bowl

plate

cupboard

fork

shower

soap

towel

bathtub

toilet

The 🪑 is in the living room.

The 🧻 is in the bathroom.

# Furniture

table

fridge

bed

shelf

chair

wardrobe

curtain

coat rack

lamp

television

armchair

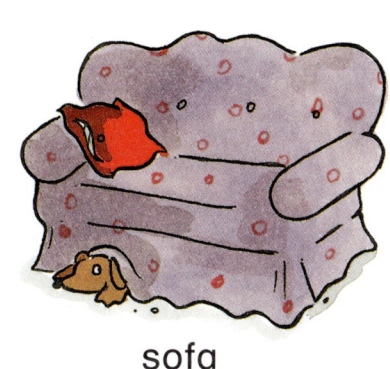

sofa

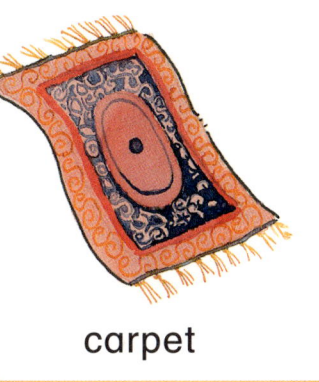

carpet

desk

Do you like this ?
Yes, I do. / No, I don't.

29

# Nature

spider

spider's web

fly

frog

flower

grass

meadow

bee

bird

bird's nest

stone

bush

river

lake

worm

ant

bug

tree

Can you see the ?
Yes, I can. / No, I can't.

# Weather

sun

cloud

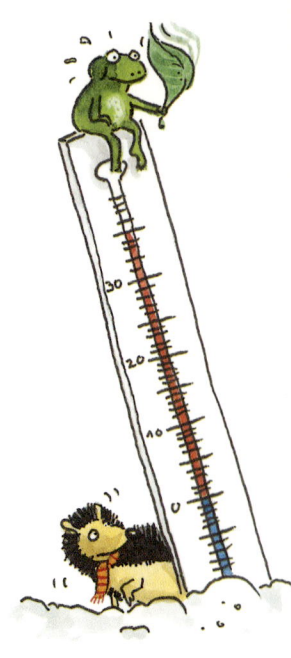
temperature

rainbow    rain

snow

lightning

thunderstorm

star

sky

fog

moon

wind

storm

How is the weather?

It's cloudy. It's stormy. It's windy.

It's rainy. It's foggy. It's sunny.

33

# Vehicles

truck

taxi

sledge

fire engine

bus

train

helicopter

plane

car

motorbike

scooter

bike

ambulance

tram

First phrases

I take the .

Look at the  !

# At School

book

pencil case

lunch box

glue

schoolbag

blackboard

watercolours

brush

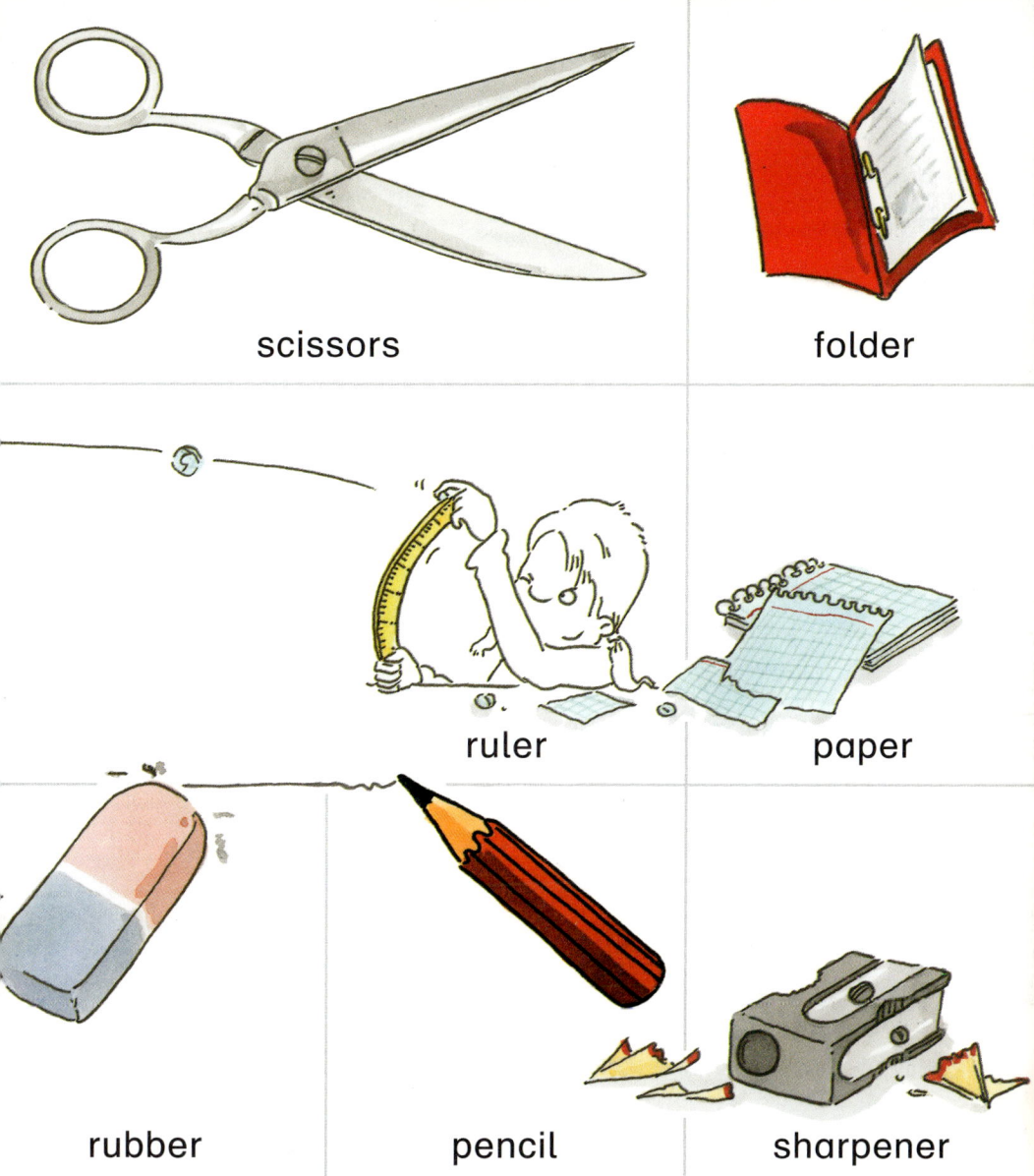

scissors

folder

ruler

paper

rubber

pencil

sharpener

Can I have the , please?

Yes, you can. / No, you can't.

# Colours and Shapes

brown

pink

white

blue

purple

yellow

red

orange

green

grey

black

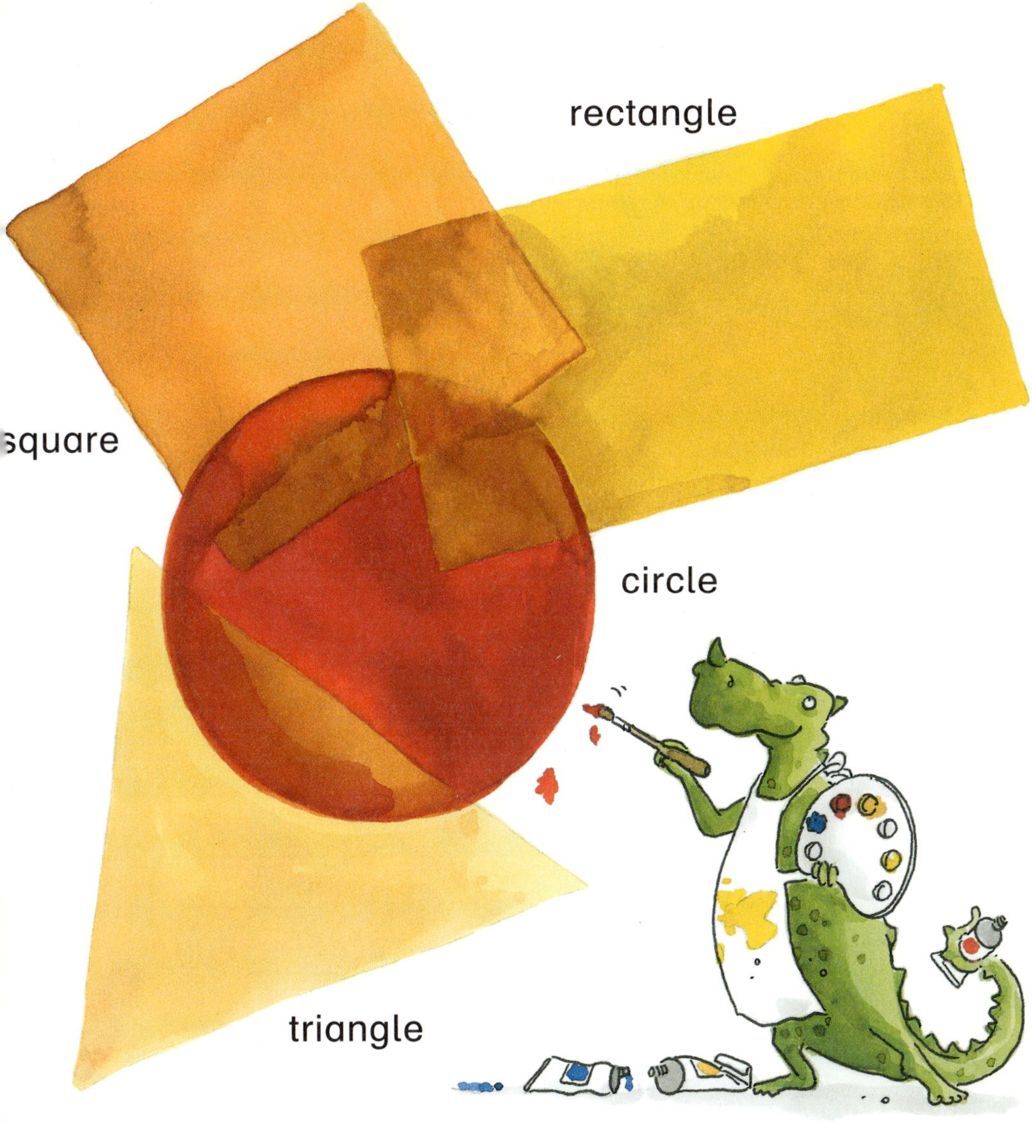

rectangle

square

circle

triangle

The  is .
The is .

39

# Numbers

five
seven
eleven
ten
nine
5
6
7
8
9
10
four
six
eight
three
4
ninety
3
two
one
2
100
one hundred
0 1
90
zero
80 eighty
50
70 60 sixty
seventy

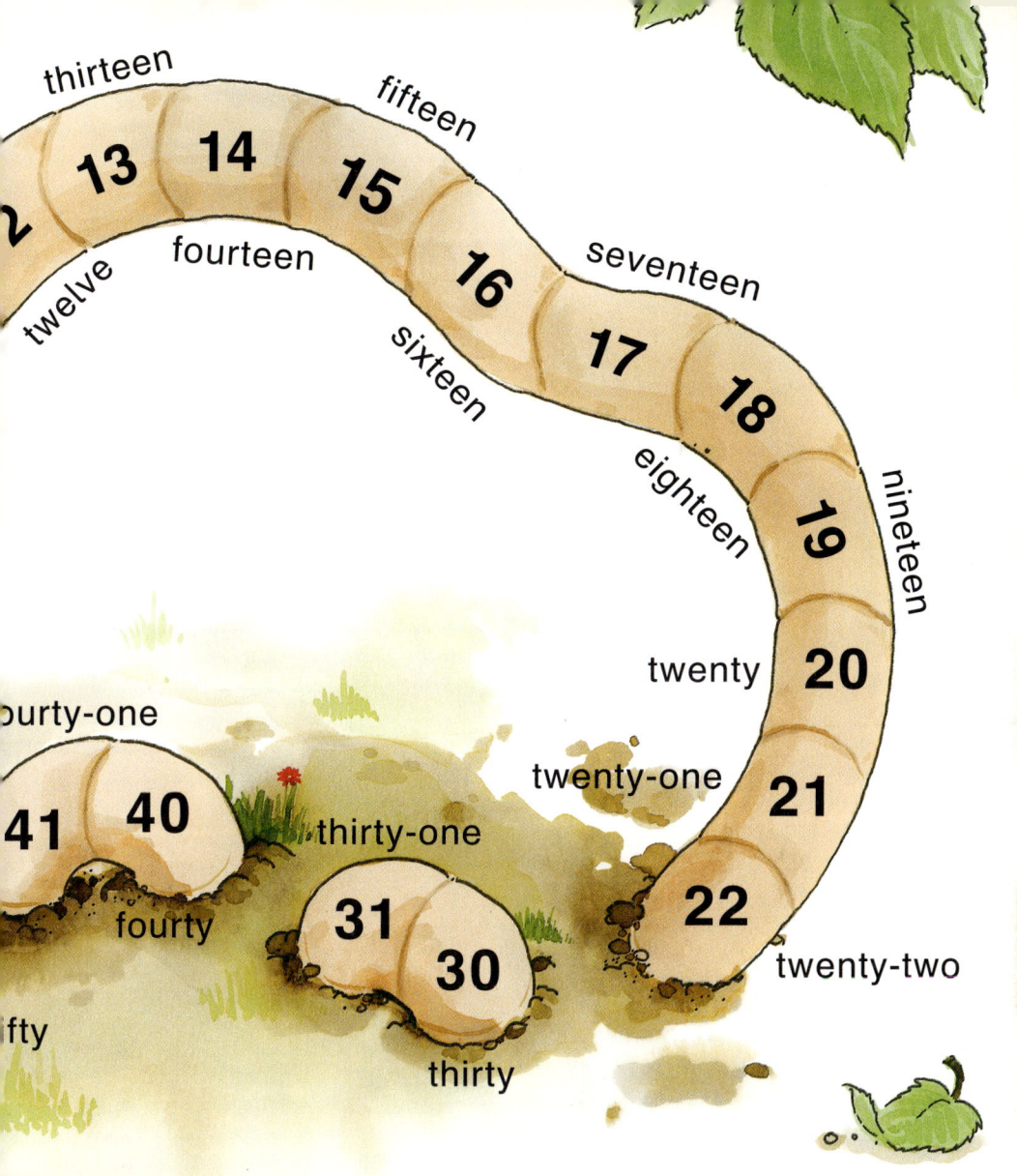

thirteen
fifteen
2 13 14 15
twelve fourteen 16 seventeen
sixteen 17
eighteen 18 nineteen
19
twenty 20
twenty-one 21
fourty-one thirty-one 22
41 40 twenty-two
fourty 31
30
fifty thirty

Please count from 4 to 12.

Please count from 11 to 5.

# Calendar

Monday

Thursday

Wednesday

Tuesday

Friday

Saturday

Sunday

spring

summer

autumn

winter

What day is it today?

Today, it's Monday.

What month is it? It's July.

# Opposites

left – right

quiet – loud

dry – wet

slow – fast

short – long

happy – sad

sweet – sour

thin – thick

dirty – clean

right – wrong

new – old

small – big

full – empty

good – bad

The opposite of  is .

is big.

# Jobs

mechanic

policeman

teacher

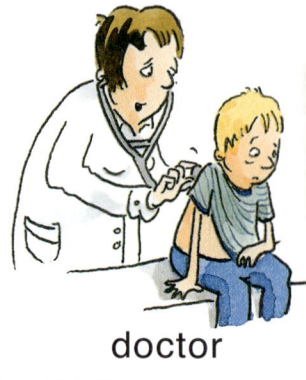

doctor

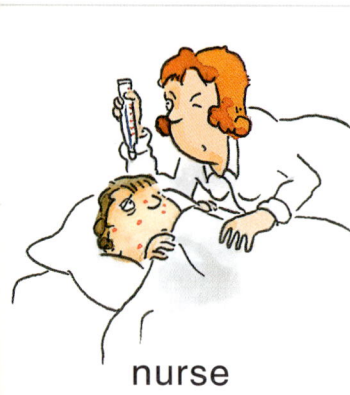

nurse

gardener

shoemaker

disc jockey

dentist

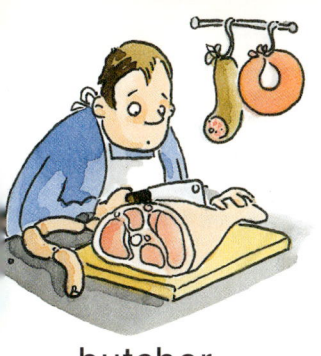

butcher

baker

cook

farmer          postman

hairdresser

fireman

Mrs Miller is a  .

Mr Miller is a .

47

# Special Days

Christmas

Halloween

pumpkin

sweets

Santa Claus

biscuit

Christmas tree

birthday party

candle

present

cake

Easter

Easter egg          Easter bunny

New Year's Eve

firework          music          balloon

Do you like Christmas?

Yes, I do. / No, I don't.

Do you like birthday parties?

49

# First Phrases (S. 8 – 27)

The monkey lives in the zoo.
The pig lives on the farm.

Where is the cat?
Here it is.

Can I have the doll, please?
Here you are.
Yes, you can. / No, you can't.

Pass the bread, please.
Here it is.

Can I have a banana, please?
Can I have some cherries, please?
Yes, you can. / No, you can't.

I like eating lettuce.
I don't like eating cauliflower.

Show me your mouth!
This is my finger.

Do you like your mother?
Yes, I do. / No, I don't.
I don't have a brother.

I like wearing my dress.
I don't like wearing my hat.

The table is in the living room.
The towel is in the bathroom.

## Erste Sätze (S. 8–27)

Der Affe lebt im Zoo.
Das Schwein lebt auf dem Bauernhof.

Wo ist die Katze?
Hier.

Kann ich bitte die Puppe haben?
Hier, bitte.
Ja. / Nein.

Reiche mir bitte das Brot.
Hier, bitte.

Bekomme ich bitte eine Banane?
Bekomme ich bitte ein paar Kirschen?
Ja. / Nein.

Ich esse gerne Salat.
Ich mag keinen Blumenkohl.

Zeige mir deinen Mund!
Das ist mein Finger.

Magst du deine Mutter?
Ja. / Nein.
Ich habe keinen Bruder.

Ich ziehe gerne mein Kleid an.
Ich setze meinen Hut nicht gerne auf.

Der Tisch steht im Wohnzimmer.
Das Handtuch ist im Badezimmer.

# First Phrases (S. 28 – 49)

Do you like this table?
Yes, I do. / No, I don't.

Can you see the frog?
Yes, I can. / No, I can't.

How is the weather?
It's cloudy. It's stormy. It's windy.
It's rainy. It's foggy. It's sunny.

I take the bus.
Look at the fire engine!

Can I have the glue, please?
Yes, you can. / No, you can't.

The tomato is red.
The banana is yellow.

Please count from 4 to 12.
Please count from 11 to 5.

What day is it today?
Today, it's Monday.
What month is it?
It's July.

The opposite of happy is sad.
Nessie is big.

Mrs Miller is a nurse.
Mr Miller is a policeman.

Do you like Christmas?
Yes, I do. / No, I don't.
Do you like birthday parties?

## Erste Sätze (S. 28–49)

Magst du diesen Tisch?
Ja. / Nein.

Siehst du den Frosch?
Ja. / Nein.

Wie ist das Wetter?
Es ist bewölkt. Es ist stürmisch. Es ist windig.
Es ist regnerisch. Es ist neblig. Es ist sonnig.

Ich fahre mit dem Bus.
Schau dir das Feuerwehrauto an!

Kann ich bitte den Klebstoff haben?
Ja. / Nein.

Die Tomate ist rot.
Die Banane ist gelb.

Bitte zähle von 4 bis 12.
Bitte zähle von 11 bis 5.

Welcher Tag ist heute?
Heute ist Montag.
Welcher Monat ist es?
Es ist Juli.

Das Gegenteil von glücklich ist traurig.
Nessie ist groß.

Frau Miller ist Krankenpflegerin.
Herr Miller ist Polizist.

Magst du Weihnachten?
Ja. / Nein.
Magst du Geburtstagsfeiern?

# Song

Good morning everybody,
how are you today?
I'm very fine, thank you,
let's go outside and play.

Skipping rope and my football,
puppets and my favourite doll,
don't forget the teddy bear,
let's take them all!

Melodie: Ein Männlein steht im Walde

# Poem

A tomato fell asleep on a railroad track,
after a while she woke up.
The five-fifteen came rushing by.
Toot! Toot! Tomato ketchup!

# Finger-play

Hello Mr Ticky Wick,
are you ready for a trick?
Can you see my little hands
with their tiny funny friends?
I can take them up and down
and can use them as a crown.

But the best thing I can do,
is – TICKLE YOU!

# Counting-out rhyme

One, two, three,
please come with me.
Four, five, six, seven, eight,
let's go to the gate.
We missed the plane,
oh, what a shame.
Let's take the car!
Out you are.

# Playtime

# Board games

# Shopping

# School

# On the way

61

# At the restaurant

# Saying goodbye

# First Phrases

## Playtime (S. 56)

| | |
|---|---|
| Come, play with me! | Komm, spiel mit mir! |
| What do you want to play? | Was willst du spielen? |
| I want to play with the building bricks. | Ich möchte mit den Bauklötzen spielen. |
| Okay, let's start. | Okay, fangen wir an. |

## Board games (S. 57)

| | |
|---|---|
| Let's set up the game! | Lass uns das Spiel aufbauen! |
| It's your turn. | Du bist dran. |
| Roll the dice. | Würfele. |
| I am the winner! | Ich habe gewonnen! |

## Eating (S. 58)

| | |
|---|---|
| I can set the table. | Ich kann den Tisch decken. |
| Do you like the soup? | Schmeckt dir die Suppe? |
| Can I have some more, please? | Kann ich bitte noch etwas bekommen? |
| Yummy, that's good! | Mmmmh, das ist lecker! |

## Shopping (S. 59)

| | |
|---|---|
| I want to buy a puppet for my friend. | Ich möchte eine Handpuppe für meinen Freund / meine Freundin kaufen. |
| How much are they? | Was kosten sie? |
| I take the witch. | Ich nehme die Hexe. |
| Here is the money. | Hier ist das Geld. |

## School (S. 60)

| | |
|---|---|
| My name is Peter. | Ich heiße Peter. |
| What's your name? | Wie heißt du? |
| Can I sit next to you? | Darf ich neben dir sitzen? |
| Do you want to play with us? | Willst du mit uns spielen? |
| Let's meet this afternoon! | Wir sollten uns heute Nachmittag treffen! |

## On the way (S. 61)

| | |
|---|---|
| Where is the bus stop? | Wo ist die Bushaltestelle? |
| Go straight on! | Gehe geradeaus! |
| Turn left! | Gehe nach links! |
| Turn right! | Gehe nach rechts! |

## At the restaurant (S. 62)

| | |
|---|---|
| Can I have the menu, please? | Kann ich bitte die Speisekarte haben? |
| I would like to have pizza with ham, please. | Ich möchte gerne Pizza mit Schinken. |
| Enjoy your meal! | Guten Appetit! |

## Saying goodbye (S. 63)

| | |
|---|---|
| Goodbye! | Auf Wiedersehen! |
| It was nice to meet you. | Schön, dass ich euch (dich) kennen gelernt habe. |
| I hope to see you again. | Ich hoffe, euch (dich) wieder-zusehen. |

| | | |
|---|---|---|
| **ambulance** ˈæmbjʊləns | Krankenwagen | **A** |
| **ant** ænt | Ameise | |
| **apple** ˈæpl | Apfel | |
| **April** ˈeɪprəl | April | |
| **arm** ɑːm | Arm | |
| **armchair** ɑːmtʃeə(r) | Sessel | |
| **August** ˈɔːgəst | August | |
| **aunt** ɑːnt | Tante | |
| **autumn** ˈɔːtəm | Herbst | |

| | | |
|---|---|---|
| **baby** ˈbeɪbɪ | Baby | **B** |
| **bad** bæd | schlecht | |
| **baker** ˈbeɪkə(r) | Bäcker/-in | |
| **ball** bɔːl | Ball | |
| **balloon** bəˈluːn | Luftballon | |
| **banana** bəˈnɑːnə | Banane | |
| **bathroom** bɑːθruːm | Badezimmer | |
| **bathtub** bɑːθtʌb | Badewanne | |
| **beans** biːnz | Bohnen | |
| **bear** beə(r) | Bär | |
| **bed** bed | Bett | |
| **bedroom** bedruːm | Schlafzimmer | |
| **bee** biː | Biene | |
| **big** bɪg | groß | |
| **bike** baɪk | Fahrrad | |
| **bird** bɜːd | Vogel | |
| **bird's nest** bɜːdz nest | Vogelnest | |
| **birthday party** bɜːθdeɪˈ pɑːtɪ | Geburtstagsfeier | |

67

| biscuit ˈbɪskɪt | Keks |
| black blæk | schwarz |
| blackboard ˈblækbɔːd | Tafel |
| blue bluː | blau |
| body ˈbɒdɪ | Körper |
| book bʊk | Buch |
| boots buːts | Stiefel |
| bowl bəʊl | Schüssel |
| bread bred | Brot |
| brother ˈbrʌðə(r) | Bruder |
| brown braʊn | braun |
| brush brʌʃ | Pinsel |
| bug bʌg | Käfer |
| building bricks ˈbɪldɪŋ brɪkz | Bauklötze |
| bus bʌs | Bus |
| bush bʊʃ | Busch |
| butcher ˈbʊtʃə(r) | Metzger/-in |
| butter ˈbʌtə(r) | Butter |

**C**

| cabbage ˈkæbɪdʒ | Kohl |
| cake keɪk | Kuchen |
| candle ˈkændl | Kerze |
| cap kæp | Mütze |
| car kɑː(r) | Auto |
| carpet ˈkɑːpɪt | Teppich |
| carrot ˈkærət | Karotte |
| cat kæt | Katze |
| cauliflower ˈkɒlɪflaʊə(r) | Blumenkohl |

| | |
|---|---|
| **chair** tʃeə(r) | Stuhl |
| **cheese** tʃiːz | Käse |
| **cherries** 'tʃerɪz | Kirschen |
| **child** tʃaɪld | Kind |
| **children** 'tʃɪldrən | Kinder |
| **chin** tʃɪn | Kinn |
| **Christmas** 'krɪsməs | Weihnachten |
| **Christmas tree** 'krɪsməs triː | Weihnachtsbaum |
| **circle** 'sɜːkl | Kreis |
| **clean** kliːn | sauber |
| **cloud** klaʊd | Wolke |
| **coat** kəʊt | Mantel |
| **coat rack** kəʊt ræk | Garderobe |
| **cook** kʊk | Koch/Köchin |
| **corn** kɔːn | Mais |
| **cow** kaʊ | Kuh |
| **cowboy** kaʊbɔɪ | Cowboy |
| **cucumber** 'kjuːkɜʌmbə(r) | Gurke |
| **cup** kʌp | Tasse |
| **cupboard** 'kʌbəd | (Küchen-)Schrank |
| **curtain** 'kɜːtən | Vorhang |

**D**

| | |
|---|---|
| **daughter** 'dɔːtə(r) | Tochter |
| **December** dɪ'sembə(r) | Dezember |
| **dentist** 'dentɪst | Zahnarzt/-ärztin |
| **desk** desk | Schreibtisch |
| **dirty** 'dɜːtɪ | schmutzig |
| **disc jockey** dɪsk dʒɔkɪ | Discjockey |

| | | |
|---|---|---|
| **doctor** 'dɒkt(r) | Arzt/Ärztin |
| **dog** dɒg | Hund |
| **doll** dɒl | Puppe |
| **dolphin** 'dɒlfɪn | Delfin |
| **door** dɔ:(r) | Tür |
| **dress** dres | Kleid |
| **dry** draɪ | trocken |
| **duck** dʌk | Ente |

**E**

| | |
|---|---|
| **ear** ɪə(r) | Ohr |
| **Easter** 'i:stə(r) | Ostern |
| **Easter bunny** 'i:stə(r) 'bʌnɪ | Osterhase |
| **Easter egg** 'i:stə(r) eg | Osterei |
| **egg** eg | Ei |
| **elbow** 'elbəʊ | Ellenbogen |
| **elephant** 'elɪfənt | Elefant |
| **empty** 'emptɪ | leer |
| **eye** aɪ | Auge |

**F**

| | |
|---|---|
| **face** feɪs | Gesicht |
| **farmer** 'fɑ:mə(r) | Landwirt/-in |
| **fast** fɑ:st | schnell |
| **father** 'fɑ:ðə(r) | Vater |
| **February** 'februərɪ | Februar |
| **finger** 'fɪŋgə(r) | Finger |
| **fire engine** 'faɪə(r) 'endʒɪn | Feuerwehrauto |
| **fireman** 'faɪə(r)mæn | Feuerwehrmann |
| **firework** 'faɪə(r) wɜ:k | Feuerwerk |

| | |
|---|---|
| **flower** flaʊə(r) | Blume |
| **fly** flaɪ | Fliege |
| **fog** fɒg | Nebel |
| **folder** ˈfəʊldə(r) | Hefter |
| **foot/feet** fʊt/fiːt | Fuß/Füße |
| **football** fʊtbɔːl | Fußball |
| **fork** fɔːk | Gabel |
| **Friday** ˈfraɪdeɪ | Freitag |
| **fridge** frɪdʒ | Kühlschrank |
| **frog** frɒg | Frosch |
| **full** fʊl | voll |

| | |
|---|---|
| **garden** gɑːdn | Garten |
| **gardener** ˈgɑːdnə(r) | Gärtner/-in |
| **ghost** gəʊst | Gespenst/Geist |
| **giraffe** dʒɪˈrɑːf | Giraffe |
| **glass** glɑːs | Glas |
| **glasses** glɑːsɪz | Brille |
| **glue** gluː | Klebstoff |
| **goat** gəʊt | Ziege |
| **goldfish** gəʊldfɪʃ | Goldfisch |
| **good** gʊd | gut |
| **goose** guːs | Gans |
| **grandfather** grændˈfɑːðə(r) | Großvater |
| **grandmother** grændˈmʌðə(r) | Großmutter |
| **grandparents** grændˈpeərənts | Großeltern |
| **grapes** greɪps | Weintrauben |

| grass | graːs | Gras |
| green | griːn | grün |
| grey | greɪ | grau |
| guinea pig | ˈgɪnɪ pɪg | Meerschweinchen |

**H**

| hair | heə(r) | Haar |
| hairdresser | heə(r)ˈdresə(r) | Friseur/-in |
| hall | hɔːl | Flur |
| Halloween | hæləʊˈiːn | Halloween |
| ham | hæm | Schinken |
| hamster | ˈhæmstə(r) | Hamster |
| hand | hænd | Hand |
| happy | ˈhæpɪ | glücklich |
| hard | hɑːd | hart |
| hat | hæt | Hut |
| head | hed | Kopf |
| helicopter | ˈhelɪkɒptə(r) | Hubschrauber |
| hen | hen | Huhn/Henne |
| honey | ˈhʌnɪ | Honig |
| horse | hɔːs | Pferd |
| hot chocolate | hɒt ˈtʃɒklət | heiße Schokolade |

**J**

| jacket | ˈdʒækɪt | Jacke |
| jam | dʒæm | Marmelade |
| January | ˈdʒænjʊərɪ | Januar |
| jigsaw puzzle | dʒɪgsɔː ˈpʌzl | Puzzle |

| | | |
|---|---|---|
| **juice** dʒuːs | Saft | |
| **July** dʒʊ'laɪ | Juli | |
| **June** dʒuːn | Juni | |

| | | |
|---|---|---|
| **king** kɪŋ | König | **K** |
| **kitchen** 'kɪtʃɪn | Küche | |
| **kite** kaɪt | Drachen | |
| **kitten** kɪtn | Kätzchen | |
| **kiwi fruit** 'kiːwiː fruːt | Kiwi | |
| **knee** niː | Knie | |
| **knife** naɪf | Messer | |

| | | |
|---|---|---|
| **lake** leɪk | See | **L** |
| **lamp** læmp | Lampe | |
| **left** left | links | |
| **leg** leg | Bein | |
| **lemon** 'lemən | Zitrone | |
| **lemonade** lemə'neɪd | Limonade | |
| **lettuce** 'letɪs | Salat | |
| **lightning** 'laɪtnɪŋ | Blitz | |
| **lion** 'laɪən | Löwe | |
| **living room** 'lɪvɪŋ ruːm | Wohnzimmer | |
| **long** lɒŋ | lang | |
| **loud** laʊd | laut | |
| **lunch box** lʌnʃ bɒks | Brotdose | |

| | | |
|---|---|---|
| **March** mɑːtʃ | März | **M** |
| **May** meɪ | Mai | |

| | | |
|---|---|---|
| **meadow** ˈmedəʊ | Wiese |
| **mechanic** mɪˈkænɪk | Mechaniker/-in |
| **milk** mɪlk | Milch |
| **mineral water** ˈmɪnərl ˈwɔːtə(r) | Mineralwasser |
| **Monday** ˈmʌndeɪ | Montag |
| **monkey** ˈmʌŋkɪ | Affe |
| **moon** muːn | Mond |
| **mother** ˈmʌðə(r) | Mutter |
| **motorbike** ˈməʊtə(r) baɪk | Motorrad |
| **mouse** maʊs | Maus |
| **mouth** maʊθ | Mund |
| **mushroom** ˈmʌʃruːm | Pilz |
| **music** ˈmjuːzɪk | Musik |

**N**

| | | |
|---|---|---|
| **neck** nek | Hals |
| **new** njuː | neu |
| **New Year's Eve** njuː jɪə(r)z iːv | Silvester |
| **nose** nəʊz | Nase |
| **November** nəˈvembə(r) | November |
| **nurse** nɜːs | Krankenpfleger/-in |

**O**

| | | |
|---|---|---|
| **October** ɒkˈtəʊbə(r) | Oktober |
| **old** əʊld | alt |
| **onion** ˈʌnjən | Zwiebel |
| **orange** ˈɒrɪndʒ | Orange/orange |

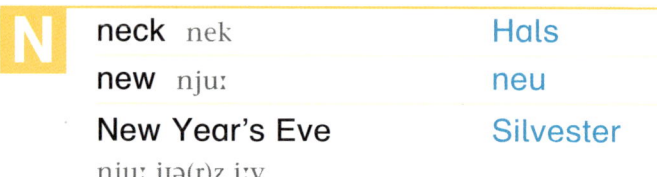

| | | |
|---|---|---|
| **paper** 'peɪpə(r) | Papier | |
| **parents** 'peərənts | Eltern | |
| **parrot** 'pærət | Papagei | |
| **peach** piːtʃ | Pfirsich | |
| **pear** peə(r) | Birne | |
| **peas** piːz | Erbsen | |
| **pen** pen | Füller | |
| **pencil** 'pensɪl | Bleistift | |
| **pencil case** 'pensɪl keɪs | Federmäppchen | |
| **penguin** 'peŋgwɪn | Pinguin | |
| **pepper** 'pepə(r) | Pfeffer | |
| **pig** pɪg | Schwein | |
| **pineapple** 'paɪnæpl | Ananas | |
| **pink** pɪŋk | pink/rosa | |
| **plane** pleɪn | Flugzeug | |
| **plate** pleɪt | Teller | |
| **play dough** pleɪ dəʊ | Knete | |
| **plum** plʌm | Pflaume | |
| **policeman** pə'liːsmən | Polizist | |
| **postman** 'pəʊstmən | Postbote | |
| **potato** pə'teɪtəʊ | Kartoffel | |
| **present** 'prezənt | Geschenk | |
| **princess** 'prɪnses | Prinzessin | |
| **pumpkin** 'pʌmpkɪn | Kürbis | |
| **puppet** 'pʌpɪt | Finger-/Handpuppe | |
| **puppy** 'pʌpɪ | Welpe | |
| **purple** 'pɜːpl | violett | |

**quiet** 'kwaɪət | leise

**R**

| rabbit 'ræbɪt | Kaninchen |
|---|---|
| radish 'rædɪʃ | Radieschen/Rettich |
| rain reɪn | Regen |
| rainbow 'reɪnbəʊ | Regenbogen |
| rectangle 'rektæŋgl | Rechteck |
| red red | rot |
| red pepper red 'pepə(r) | roter Paprika |
| right raɪt | rechts/richtig |
| river 'rɪvə(r) | Fluss |
| rubber 'rʌb(r) | Radiergummi |
| ruler 'ruːlə(r) | Lineal |

**S**

| sad sæd | traurig |
|---|---|
| salt sɔːlt | Salz |
| Santa Claus 'sæntə klɔːz | Weihnachtsmann |
| Saturday 'sætədeɪ | Samstag |
| schoolbag skuːlbæg | Schulranzen |
| scissors 'sɪzəz | Schere |
| scooter 'skuːt(r) | Motorroller |
| September sep'tembə(r) | September |
| sharpener 'ʃɑːpnə(r) | Bleistiftspitzer |
| sheep ʃiːp | Schaf |
| shelf ʃelf | Bord/Regal |
| shirt ʃɜːt | Hemd |
| shoemaker ʃuː'meɪk(r) | Schuhmacher/-in |
| shoes ʃuːz | Schuhe |
| short ʃɔːt | kurz |
| shorts ʃɔːts | Shorts |

a b c d e f g h i j k l m n o p q r s t v w x y z

| | | |
|---|---|---|
| **shoulder** ˈʃəʊldə(r) | Schulter |
| **shower** ˈʃaʊə(r) | Dusche |
| **sister** ˈsɪstə(r) | Schwester |
| **skipping rope** ˈskɪpɪŋ rəʊp | Springseil |
| **skirt** skɜːt | Rock |
| **sky** skaɪ | Himmel |
| **sledge** sledʒ | Schlitten |
| **slow** sləʊ | langsam |
| **small** smɔːl | klein |
| **snow** snəʊ | Schnee |
| **soap** səʊp | Seife |
| **socks** sɒks | Socken |
| **sofa** ˈsəʊfə | Sofa |
| **son** sʌn | Sohn |
| **sour** ˈsaʊə(r) | sauer |
| **spider** ˈspaɪdə(r) | Spinne |
| **spider's web** ˈspaɪdə(r)s web | Spinnennetz |
| **spoon** spuːn | Löffel |
| **spring** sprɪŋ | Frühling |
| **square** skweə(r) | Quadrat |
| **stairway** steə(r)weɪ | Treppe |
| **star** stɑː(r) | Stern |
| **stone** stəʊn | Stein |
| **storm** stɔːm | Sturm |
| **strawberries** ˈstrɔːbərɪz | Erdbeeren |
| **sugar** ˈʃʊgə(r) | Zucker |
| **summer** ˈsʌmə(r) | Sommer |

| | | |
|---|---|---|
| **sun** sʌn | Sonne |
| **Sunday** ˈsʌndeɪ | Sonntag |
| **sunglasses** sʌnɡlɑːsɪz | Sonnenbrille |
| **sweater** ˈswetə(r) | Pullover |
| **sweet** swiːt | süß |
| **sweets** swiːts | Süßigkeiten |

**T**

| | | |
|---|---|---|
| **table** ˈteɪbl | Tisch |
| **taxi** ˈtæksɪ | Taxi |
| **tea** tiː | Tee |
| **teacher** ˈtiːtʃə(r) | Lehrer/-in |
| **teddy bear** ˈtedɪ beə(r) | Teddybär |
| **television** telɪˈvɪʒn | Fernseher |
| **temperature** ˈtemprɪtʃə(r) | Temperatur |
| **thick** θɪk | dick |
| **thin** θɪn | dünn |
| **thumb** θʌm | Daumen |
| **thunderstorm** ˈθʌndə(r)stɔːm | Gewitter |
| **Thursday** ˈθɜːzdeɪ | Donnerstag |
| **tiger** ˈtaɪɡə(r) | Tiger |
| **toe** təʊ | Zehe |
| **toilet** ˈtɔɪlɪt | Toilette/Gäste-WC |
| **tomato** təˈmɑːtəʊ | Tomate |
| **tongue** tʌŋ | Zunge |
| **tooth/teeth** tuːθ/tiːθ | Zahn/Zähne |
| **towel** ˈtaʊəl | Handtuch |
| **train** treɪn | Zug |

**78**

| | | |
|---|---|---|
| **train set** treɪn set | Spielzeugeisenbahn | |
| **tram** træm | Straßenbahn | |
| **tree** triː | Baum | |
| **triangle** ˈtraɪæŋgl | Dreieck | |
| **trousers** ˈtraʊzəz | Hose | |
| **truck** trʌk | Lastwagen | |
| **Tuesday** ˈtjuːzdeɪ | Dienstag | |
| **turtle** tɜːtl | Schildkröte | |
| **twins** twɪnz | Zwillinge | |

| | | |
|---|---|---|
| **uncle** ˈʌŋkl | Onkel | **U** |

| | | |
|---|---|---|
| **wardrobe** ˈwɔːdrəʊb | Kleiderschrank | **W** |
| **watch** wɒtʃ | Uhr | |
| **watercolours** ˈwɔːtə(r)ˈkʌlə(r)z | Wasserfarben | |
| **watermelon** ˈwɔːtə(r)ˈmelən | Wassermelone | |
| **Wednesday** ˈwenzdeɪ | Mittwoch | |
| **wet** wet | nass | |
| **white** waɪt | weiß | |
| **wind** wɪnd | Wind | |
| **window** ˈwɪndəʊ | Fenster | |
| **winter** ˈwɪntə(r) | Winter | |
| **witch** wɪtʃ | Hexe | |
| **worm** wɜːm | Wurm | |
| **wrong** rɒŋ | falsch | |

| | | |
|---|---|---|
| **yellow** ˈjeləʊ | gelb | **Y** |

# Lautschrifttabelle

| | | | | | | |
|---|---|---|---|---|---|---|
| ɑː | wie in warm | arm | | ei | | Monday |
| e | wie in Fleck | egg | | əʊ | | pony |
| iː | wie in Wiese | knee | | r | | rabbit |
| i | wie in Baby | puppy | | ʒ | | television |
| ɪ | wie in Tisch | pig | | θ | | tooth |
| ɒ | wie in Frosch | frog | | ð | | father |
| ʊ | wie in Hund | foot | | w | | water-melon |
| uː | wie in Blume | room | | | | |
| ə | wie in Mutter | mother | | b | | banana |
| aɪ | wie in Kleid | bike | | d | | doll |
| aʊ | wie in blau | cow | | f | | fish |
| ɔɪ | wie in neu | toy | | g | | garden |
| ɪə | wie in Tier | ear | | h | | hand |
| eə | wie in Meer | hair | | j | | yellow |
| ŋ | wie in Ballon | long | | k | | cap |
| s | wie in Skelett | sofa | | l | | lemon |
| z | wie in Salat | zoo | | m | | milk |
| ʃ | wie in Schule | shirt | | n | | nose |
| tʃ | wie in tschüss | child | | p | | pink |
| dʒ | wie in Dschungel | juice | | t | | taxi |
| v | wie in Vampir | van | | | | |
| æ | fast wie in Bär | bat | | | | |
| ɔ | fast wie in Horn | doll | | | | |
| ʌ | fast wie in Stadt | puppet | | | | |
| ʒ | fast wie in stört | bird | | | | |

Diese Laute gibt es nur im Englischen.

wie im Deutschen